DISCLAIMER

If you've never eaten something described in this book, only eat a small amount of it the first time, just in case you are allergic. I've done my best to cover antinutrients, possibly to the point of overkill, but that doesn't mean I've covered EVERYTHING, so do your research with unfamiliar species.

Be safe and have fun experimenting!

Thanks to my favorite human Anna McCambridge-Thomas who helped proofread this book and put up with sooo many messes in the kitchen.
Thanks to everyone who has given me cool edible plants over the years, there are so many of you. Josh Jamison especially.
Thanks to Gus Ramage for sharing so much surplus produce from your home garden with me.

And thanks to my parents, who put up with me taking over their yard with edible plants when I was just starting to learn about all this stuff.

CONTENTS

CUISINE – 3
Part ONE: NUTRITION
Staple crops – 4
Fat/other vegetables – 5
Leaves – 6
Fruit – 7
Nutrients/antinutrients – 8
PART TWO: HYPERPALATABILITY – 9
Taste – 10
Aromatics – 11
Flavor – 12
Cooking – 13
Ferment – 14
Size & shape – 15
Bits – 16
Strings – 17
Fresh batter – 18
Flour – 19
Bread – 20
Sourdough – 22
Some bread – 23
Mouthfeel – 24
Chewy/meaty/dense – 25
Sauce/soup – 26
A sauce – 27
PART THREE: INGREDIENT MANIPULATIONS
Sweet potato – 28
Cassava – 29
Yam – 30
Musa – 32
Xanthosoma/taro – 33
Cowpea – 34
Pumpkin – 35
Papaya – 36
Leaves – 37
Shoots – 38
Leaf powder – 39
PART FOUR: PUTTING IT ALL TOGETHER
Nutritional balance/hyperpalatable contrast – 41
Make YOUR cuisine – 42
Everything all the time – 43
Some ideas – 44

WHAT THIS BOOK IS:

Brute force techniques for preparing food out of what you are growing in your HUMID SUBTROPICAL MULTISTORY HOMEGARDEN. The foods described within are being grown in central Florida, but the ideas and techniques should be applicable elsewhere, just with different species. Starch is starch, leaves are leaves, fat is fat anywhere around the world. (pretty much)

NOTE: There are no universal this-is-positively-what-will-happen instructions in this book. Each species you work with is going to be different. All species of yam do not behave in exactly the same way. All varieties of a single species of yam do not behave exactly the same way.

This book gives you a rough sketch of how the ingredients behave, but it will be up to you to experiment with how the particular type of yam that grows well in your particular patch of land will transform when you turn it into food.

This book is about diversity and uniqueness. The food you make won't turn out like the food they make the next city over. It shouldn't even be like the food they are making in the neighborhood next to you. It's probably going to be different than your next-door-neighbors food.

This is HOMEGARDEN CUISINE. A cuisine based on what grows well right outside of your house. Food you can live off of that likes to grow where you live.

Also, there are FAR more options for ingredients than are listed in this book. Figure out what grows best where you live and grow and eat that.

NUTRITION
making food that is good for you

CALORIES
KEEPING YOUR BODY RUNNING

Warm blooded animals tend to need quite a bit of these, quite frequently. You can get calories from a wide variety of sources, but this book is going to focus on getting the bulk of calories from tuber and fruit starches, with seeds, fruit, and oil as secondary sources.

FAT
DELICIOUS AND ESSENTIAL

FAT is an essential part of the human diet. Fats described in this book will be seed and fruit oils, cold pressed as needed to preserve fat quality.

— THE FOODS YOUR ANCESTORS SURVIVED ON —

PROTEIN
AMINO ACIDS

The main protein sources described in this book are legumes and leaves.

VITAMINS & MINERALS
HEALTHY GOODSTUFF

Edible leaves have the highest concentration of vitamins & minerals, with fresh fruit coming in 2nd.*

*Besides animal products

CUISINE
The most NUTRITIONAL and HYPERPALATABLE diet that can be grown WELL in a particular region. This book is about the HUMID SUBTROPICS

HYPERPALATABILITY
making food that is delicious

TASTE
tongue effects

AROMATICS
nose happiness

— SUPERNORMAL VERSIONS OF THE FOODS YOUR ANCESTORS ATE —

FLAVOR
nose & tongue teamup

TEXTURE
keeping the mouth entertained

PART ONE: NUTRITION

PRIMARY CALORIES
the most productive crops*

What about corn, rice, wheat and potatoes? The foods that built civilizations? The foods that increased our population to gazillions? Sorry, this is a FOOD book, not a philosophy book. Anyway, I don't think you need ANOTHER book about how to make wheat bread or corn syrup. Go read those other books if you want to know about the Big Four.

CASSAVA — manihot esculenta
productive, easy to grow, prone to falling over. takes about 8-12 months to get a harvest. You can leave the roots in the ground longer, but they might get woody.

DIOSCOREA alata, d. bulbifera*
YAM
Productive, pretty much care free. Vines need support.
d. rotundata, d. cayenensis, d. esculenta
d. pentaphylla, d. polystachya **
* Difficult to grow in FL now. Only eat edible cultivars!
** I haven't had much success with this species.

SWEET POTATO
ipomoea batatas
Usually carefree the first year grown. Try and rotate with other crops to avoid a build up of pests. (I would rotate ALL your staples) If you need to cut back the rampant vines, eat the leaves & shoot tips!

BANANA
MUSA spp
(used unripe)
Plantain & "cooking" types might have more amylose starch, but you can use the mature green fruit of any variety as a staple starch.

STAPLE CROPS
The most STORABLE CALORIES you can grow per area of sunlight
The backbone of any cuisine consists of the high calorie crops that keep us warm blooded animals alive.

SECONDARY CALORIES
Other starchy staple crops. These are usually less productive than the Primary staples, but still provide a good amount of calories and diversity in the diet.

taro
Colocasia esculenta
Some varieties require wetland soil conditions

malanga (tends to have a stronger flavor than the other staples)
Xanthosoma sagitifolium & spp

POTATO MINT
plectranthus rotundifolius
Very similar in taste to solanum potato, just smaller. There are also other tuberous mint species to try!

LEGUMES
Phaseolus spp, Cajanus cajan, lablab purpureus
Annual & Perennial
psophocarpus tetragonolobus etc.

** I do like potatoes though. I just don't have much experience growing them, so they won't be included in this book.

MAXIMIZING CALORIES

LEAST CALORIES → MORE CALORIES → MAX

RAW - provides the minimal amount of digestable calories

COOKED - food is more digestable, more calories are absorbed.

GROUND TO A POWDER THEN COOKED - the maximum amount of calories can now be absorbed. (if that's what you want)

HONORABLE mention
CANNA EDULIS
a good staple if you can find a PRODUCTIVE variety.

FAT

Fat is a really important part of the diet. Not only is it essential for our survival, but it also makes food taste delicious. I don't yet have a good handle on growing my own fat yet, but I am experimenting with the species below.

MORINGA
Mature moringa seeds are BITTER, but the OIL is DELICIOUS!

TIGER NUTS
Productive, but well loved by animals who like to harvest them the day before you intended to harvest them.

PEANUTS

AVOCADO*
avocado oil is a great cooking oil. However, whole avocado flesh becomes bitter if cooked.
*if you can avoid laurel wilt

MACADAMIA

PUMPKIN
(high in omega 6 fatty acids. Should be used fresh, and not heated too much.)

There are lots of other options like perilla frutescens, olives, pachira aquatica, palms, pines, etc that could be used as oil sources. I know, I have a lot of work to do. Animal fat is another healthy option.

OTHER VEGETABLES
LOWER CALORIE than STAPLE CROPS, BUT STILL GOOD FOOD. A few suggestions are listed below. You could also grow some ANNUAL vegetables, if you are into that sort of thing.

Young cucurbits — chayote, tindora, loofa, pumpkin, bittermelon, etc.

SHOOT TIPS

MILD PEPPERS

perennial solanums

STEMS — amaranth, banana, galangal, celery stem, taro, etc

FLOWERS

green papaya
unripe mango
unripe spondias
unripe jackfruit

YOUNG morrenia odorata

cactus pads (OK, these are technically LEAVES but they are THICK leaves.)

YOUNG BEANPODS

YOUNG KATUK FRUIT & moringa pods

STACHYS

etc etc etc

LEAVES

THE MOST VITAMINS / MINERALS / PROTEIN for the LEAST AMOUNT of CALORIES. There are SO MANY options for edible leaf species. You really have no excuse for not including a diverse and abundant amount of them in your diet.

CHAYA
chidoscolus aconitifolius

- leaves and tender shoot tips contain HCN, so boil at least 5 minutes before eating.

MULBERRY
morus alba

- Some varieties have better texture than others, but all the ones I've tried taste delicious cooked. (raw not so much.)

KATUK
sauropus androgynus

Potentially dangerous RAW in high quantities. I blanch young leaves and shoots. Cook older leaves longer.

MORINGA
moringa stenopetala
moringa oleifera

SHOOTS and LEAVES are pretty extreme tasting RAW, but cooking, fermenting, or drying them makes them delicious

SWEET POTATO
ipomoea batatas

extremely tender leaves & shoots need minimal cooking or they dissolve into goop.

PUMPKIN
cucurbita moschata

LEAVES & SHOOTS COOKED

TINDORA
coccinia grandis

CHAYOTE
sechium edule

TARO
colocasia esculenta
colocasia gigantea (Bacha)

Some leaf varieties have less raphides than tuber varieties ALWAYS COOK!

XANTHOSOMA
xanthosoma brasiliense
x. saggitifolium

species & cultivars will have different amounts of raphides ALWAYS COOK!

AMARANTHS
amaranthus spp

BIDENS PILOSA

BOILING is recommended.

gynura crepioides
gynura procumbens

tasty raw, these disintegrate quickly if cooked.

HAITIAN BASKET VINE
trichostigma octandrum

Cook the leaves & shoots. Young leaves are excellent.

EDIBLE LEAF LEGUMES
lablab purpureus
winged bean
cowpea
lima bean

COOK THESE

EDIBLE LEAF "WEEDS"

There are so MANY edible wild greens. Learn and eat what grows where you live!

ANNUAL LEAF VEG.

In the colder parts of the year it can be nice to grow annual greens while the perennials have slowed their growth.

+ HUNDREDS of OTHER SPECIES

SERIOUSLY, it would fill up another book to list them all.

fruit

Seasonal treats, sauces, condiments, drinks. Candy with vitamins and minerals.

SOUR

unripe sweet fruit

kaffir lime
sour orange
SOUR CITRUS
calamondin
limequat
(can be tricky to grow in FL)

SUMAC
rhus copallinum

SWEET/SOUR

pineapple

eugenia spp.

MULBERRIES
morus spp

MYSORE RASPBERRY
rubus niveus

STARFRUIT
averrhoa carambola

TAMARIND
tamarindus indica

SPONDIAS spp

BLUEBERRIES
vaccinium spp.

SWEET

RIPE BANANAS
musa spp

MANGO
mangifera indica

MUNTINGIA
muntingia calabura

BLACK SAPOTE
diospyros nigra

WHITE SAPOTE
casimiroa edulis

PERSIMMON
diospyros kaki

PAPAYA
carica papaya

PLUS HUNDREDS of OTHER SPECIES

What about protein?

Eat 2000 calories of leaves, seeds, tubers, fruit, shoots, flowers, bulbs, and rhizomes everyday and you'll probably get enough protein. But see below.

THIS IS NOT A COMPLETE DIET!

It is missing some things like B12, vitamin D (get some sun!) much selenium, much omega 3 fatty acids, or iodine, or excessive amounts of protein. You will probably want to supplement with other whole foods like fish, eggs, insects, fungi, snails, dairy, etc. This book will not be talking about these foods because my home garden is currently deficient in them. SORRY!

BOOSTING NUTRIENTS

Fermentation of vegetables (including seeds) can increase levels of B vitamins, vitamin C, and even protein in some ferments. It is probably a good idea to eat some fermented food.

ANTINUTRIENTS

AKA: nobody likes being eaten or having their children eaten. But everyone has to eat, so here are some ways to get around plant defenses.

RAPHIDES
broken-glass-like bits of calcium oxalate found in taro & malanga leaves & tubers.

Cooking the tubers makes the raphides inert so they won't hurt your mouth (but apparently the calcium oxalate is still there.) Boiling leaves (leaves) the oxalate in the cooking water. I usually test a tiny bit, chewing & spitting out to make sure raphides are null.

PHYTOHEMAGGLUTININS
unhelpful proteins found in some legumes, kidney and lima beans especially.

COOK COMPLETELY

I don't make kidney or lima bean flour, just in case I don't fully cook the phytohem. while making pancakes or something quick. But then again, you can buy lima bean flour, so it might be ok.

OXALIC ACID
can potentially combine with calcium to form kidney stones.

It is found in so MANY foods, and probably isn't anything to worry about unless you are living off unripe starfruit and sorrel salads.

EAT DIVERSE and you should be OK.

HYDROGEN CYANIDE (HCN)
found in cassava & chaya. smaller amounts cook out, larger amounts need fermentation.

peel and leaves contain the most HCN in cassava

Some cultivars have more HCN than others.

(Eat moderate amounts of a whole bunch of different species!)

AFLATOXIN
toxins made by certain molds. If you are not intentionally growing mold, don't eat mold.

PHYTIC ACID
found in many seeds, it binds to minerals, making them unabsorbable.
SOAK/FERMENT or germinate

DETOX

SOAKING
under water

a 48 hour soak greatly reduces HCN & oxalates.

FERMENTATION
under water removes even more HCN, oxalates, phytic acid.

(soaking leads to fermentation)
→ all seeds should probably be soaked, or better yet fermented

COOKING
gets rid of any remaining anti-nutrients after soaking/fermenting.

DIVERSITY
Eating a whole bunch of just ONE thing is just asking for trouble, especially when you are eating plants, whose only defense is to try and poison you before you eat too much of them.

EAT DIVERSE!

PART TWO
HYPERPALATABILITY
excessively palatable food

Hyperpalatable food is a SUPERNORMAL STIMULUS: an exaggerated version of food that we crave even more than we desire normal food. We have evolved to enjoy food that is sweet, fatty, salty, chewy, crunchy, easy to chew and digest, with a bit of sour, not too much. The food with the most reward for the least effort. A SUPERNORMAL version of this is food that is EXTREMELY sweet, fatty, salty, chewy, crunchy, easy to chew and digest, with a dash of sour to balance things out. ALL AT ONCE. Food that hits all the dopamine inducing notes at the same time, as loudly as possible.

What tastes good to you is based on three things:

1.) Childhood foods you ate. (What your mum ate when she was pregnant with you and breastfeeding you, and what you enjoyed eating when you were a wee human.
2.) Nutritional needs (calories, protein, fats, vitamins & minerals.)
3.) Foods that allowed your ancestors to survive tend to taste great.

SUPERNORMAL versions of these foods taste EVEN BETTER.

Everything you learned in 1.) can be changed. It might be difficult, but you can learn to love foods that you did not eat when you were growing up. (aversion to bitterness might be more difficult to change.)

You WILL crave supernormal food once you have experienced it. If you have ever gone to a restaurant or bought processed food at a grocery store, you have experienced supernormally stimulating food.

You have a couple of options to deal with your craving.

1.) Ignore the junkfood.
2.) Make supernormal HYPERPALATABLE food at home with ingredients from your homegarden.
  The trick is to make slightly-but-not-too-supernormal foods that are also nutritionally sound and good for your health.

THIS IS HOMEGARDEN CUISINE

primates love sweetness

SWEET RIPE FRUIT, SUGAR CANE

SOUR FRUIT (ripe & unripe) — vitamin C!

LACTIC ACID fermentation

SWEET

SOUR

STEVIA

sweet potato

miracle fruit (makes acidic foods sweet!)

acetic acid (vinegar fermentation)

SOUR LEAVES — oxalic and other acids including vitamin C

taste

The most DELICIOUS meals are those that hit ALL the taste notes. Most of the staple crops are a bit bland on their own, so you can make them more HYPERPALATABLE using ingredients on this page in sauces, marinades, blends or layers.

A good number of edible leaves and vegetables are bitter. This is probably because plants don't really want you to eat them. Unfortunately for plants, humans have figured out that bitterness is often bundled with lots of vitamins, minerals and protein. It is worthwhile to cultivate a taste for bitterness.

BITTER

Bitter leaves

On its own, bitterness can be hard to enjoy, but combined with salt, fat, sweetness, sourness, it can add another layer of complexity to the meal.

Cooking, even just a 30 second blanch, tends to reduce bitterness dramatically.

BITTER VEGETABLES

THE TASTE of FREE AMINO ACIDS.

UMAMI

fermented beans

Usually found in foods where the proteins are starting to breakdown into free amino acids.

yeast

SALTY

HALOPHYTES   SALT (go to the ocean)

MINT FAMILY
mint, rosemary, thyme, oregano, sage, basil, cuban oregano, lemon balm, perilla, vietnamese balm, bee balm, (moujean tea) etc etc etc

LIPPIA, LEMON VERBENA - VERBENA FAMILY

GINGER FAMILY
ginger, turmeric, galangal, etc

ALLIUM FAMILY
garlic chives, onion chives, bunching onion, society garlic, etc.

PEPPERS
hot, mild, seasoning, etc.

CURRY TREE

CITRUS FAMILY *
calamondin, limequat, kaffir lime, trifoliate orange, etc.
* good luck

PIPER FAMILY
black pepper, root beer plant, betel leaf, piper sarmentosum, etc.

MYRTLE family
all spice, lemon, bay rum, etc

LAUREL family
cinnamon, persea, sassafras, bay laurel

PANDAN

LEMONGRASS

marigold
lemon desert marigold, mexican tarragon

a few options

AROMATICS

Is it edible? Does it smell nice or interesting? If yes it is an aromatic.

There are gazzillions of options. Don't ever feel limited by the few types of herbs and spices you can buy in the shops. There are soooo many other scents out there to discover. Experiment with everything until you learn what you like, and what grows well where you live. Your aromatic blends will be as unique as your home garden!

Aromatics are usually volatile, thats why you smell them, because they escape into the air easily and go up your nose. This is great, except that when the odor goes into the air, IT IS LOST. And the more odor that goes into the air the less there is in the food itself (this is why old herbs & spices don't smell as powerful as they did when they were fresh.) Generally you want to release these aromatic compounds INSIDE YOUR MOUTH instead of into the air of the kitchen, nice as that is.

To do this, you will want to:

CAPTURE AROMATICS
in hot or cold oil, or vinegar
(most aromatic compounds are fat soluble, and are not easily captured in water)

or add a small amount of raw aromatics to food moments before serving

AMPLIFY & COMPLICATE

MAILLARD REACTION
amino acids + sugars @ 280-330F
= HUNDREDS of FLAVOR COMPOUNDS

(COOKING AT HIGH TEMPERATURES
BROWNING REACTIONS
MAKES FOOD MORE DELICIOUS)

CARAMELIZATION
SUGARS @ 230-356°F
= NEW COMPLEX FLAVORS

FERMENTATION
sugars → yeast → alcohol → bacteria → FLAVORS → acetic acid

The digestion of plants by bacteria & yeasts releases a lot of complex flavors from amino acids, fatty acids, sulphur compounds, and more.

sugars → bacteria → FLAVORS ← lactic acid

FLAVOR
TASTE + AROMATICS

Combining delicious smelling AROMATICS with sweet/sour/salty/umami/bitter/fatty will give you flavorful food. However, to make your cuisine even more HYPERPALATABLE, you can use a few tricks to wring out even MORE FLAVOR!

DEHYDRATION
INTENSIFY flavor by removing water

FRESH RAW INGREDIENTS
flavorful compounds in plants that have not oxidized yet tend to have the most KICK. Add at the last minute before serving.

FAT
adding fat pretty much makes EVERYTHING more delicious.

SPECIAL FX

COOLING menthol

HEAT capsaicin

TINGLING spilanthol & zanthoxylum spp

AROMATIC SMOKE

PRESSURE COOKER
Cooks food faster & at higher temps than regular boiling/steaming. Great for beans, tough leaves, tubers. Can reach 250°F for BROWNING REACTIONS.
BOIL to remove Anti-NUTRIENTS STEAM to retain NUTRIENTS.

POTLIKKER
Save the liquid from boiled greens to use in soups, breads & sauces, or drinks.
(*except high oxalate greens like taro, or greens where the cooking water should be discarded)

AQUAFABA
The liquid from boiled beans. Use like POTLIKKER or boil down to thicken to use as an egg substitute. (Foams, binder)

The water from boiled pumpkins or sweet potato makes a delicious drink. You can ferment with kefir for sourness, or use as POTLIKKER

After soaking 24 hours, I cook dry beans @ pressure for 20 minutes.

I use 3/4 to 1 cup water per cup of beans in the pressure cooker

BLANCHING
in boiling water or steam, then quickly cooling in cold water is my favorite way to cook tender leaves and shoots.
★ BOIL CHAYA at least 5 min
★ BOIL raphide species until they don't irritate your mouth
★ Cassava leaves have variable levels of HCN that will need to be cooked out.

Steaming is probably the most forgiving cooking method.

STACKABLE STEAMER
REALLY USEFUL for steamed breads (and vegetables)

Hard-to-peel yams, bananas, taro, can be cooked with peel ON, then the peel can be more easily removed before eating

BAKING TIMES
depend on the thickness of what you are baking. A WHOLE intact sweet potato will take longer to cook than that same sweet potato cut up into peices and cooked in a flat layer.

400°F for 45 min

400°F for 30 min

APPROXIMATE BAKING TIMES @ 400°F
DRIER FOOD COOKS FASTER / WETTER FOOD COOKS SLOWER

45-60 min	30-45 min	15-30 min	10-15 min	10 min
LARGE WHOLE TUBERS*	MEDIUM TUBERS	SMALL TUBERS	TINY BITS	TINY FLAT BITS

COOKING

*and supernormal tubers called "BREAD"

I like to ferment leaves that are high in oxalic acid, like moringa. This also improves the flavor of the raw leaves.

ADD approx 1-3 TBS SALT per quart. You will start out with what looks like a very large amount of leaves but after massaging, that amount will shrink dramatically

after massaging with salt, liquid will start to come out of the leaves. When you pack this into jars, make sure the leaves are completely submerged under this liquid. (you can add a bit of water if you need to) Let this ferment until it gets as sour as you like.

FERMENT!

Purely SWEET fruit like bananas and papaya can be fermented for complex acidity. The amount of time you let the fruit ferment will determine the sweet/sour balance.

liquid tends to separate from floating pulp in a fermented puree

After the pulp separates from the liquid, you can separate it with a strainer

pulp, dehydrate into sour chewy bits, or use in breads, etc.

A NICE sweet/sour drink

OR you can blend this back together for a nice sauce base

NOTE: FRUIT PUREE EXPANDS while fermenting.

DON'T OVERFILL FERMENT CONTAINER! STIR thick purees frequently to discourage molds, or use a floating cover that keeps out air but allows expansion. jumpstarting with kefir can help too.

fermented mango puree

Keep whatever you are fermenting SUBMERGED under liquid using a non-porous weight.

KEFIR is handy to keep around for jumpstarting ferments, including sourdough

KEFIR will ferment a wide variety of carbs. this is a soft gel made from kefir fermented AQUAFABA

PUMPKIN POTLIKKER fermented with kefir makes a delicious drink. (or sauce base, bread liquid)

You can also jumpstart ferments with edible flowers, fruits, fruit peels and tuber peels. You can strain these out after fermenting.

CARBONATED SODAS can be made by fermenting sweet fruit juice/puree or sugarcane juice in a container that can handle the pressure without exploding.

I use this:

E-Z cap releases too much pressure

PLASTIC SODA BOTTLE

SIZE & SHAPE

Starting with raw ingredients, you can shape your food any way you like. This can add diversity to meals when you have an overabundance of any particular ingredient.

BUT PLEASE KEEP YOUR DIET AS DIVERSE AS POSSIBLE!

LEAF STRIPS

SPIRAL CUTTER for hard vegetables or hard fruit. → raw noodles → BLANCHED noodles (30 second boil or steam, dunked in cold water to cool)

stir fried with oil

17

STRINGS

I have no idea why humans enjoy eating strings (supernormal grubs? worms?)
The trick to making noodles is making a dough that is STRONG enough to hold together while the starches gelatinize in hot water or steam. Then you have to remove the noodles from the heat before the starches overcook and disintegrate.
Use BOILING liquid and as MUCH flour as you can get away with to make the STRONGEST DOUGH.

1-2 parts flour +
1 part liquid (room temp / warm / boiling)

extrude with ricer or noodle press

COOK in simmering water until noodles float. (this usually happens pretty fast.) This method is less forgiving of overcooking than steaming.

dehydrate before or after cooking for storable noodles.

Use MORE flour to make a DENSE dough for rolled/cut noodles.
Use boiling liquid with enough flour to make a playdough texture for extruding.

Colder liquid and less flour can be used if steaming. → KNEAD the DOUGH until it gets nice & smooth

A finer ground flour makes more cohesive noodles.

1.) removed @ float (30 sec) - pretty good. 2.) Simmered 1 minute - a little soggy 3.) Simmered 2 minutes - getting mushy
(overcooking tuber starches is easy)

roll out and cut into strips

NEAR-BOIL OR STEAM
(thicker noodles can handle a low boil, thinner noodles need a calmer simmer)

holding noodles like this above steam until they break off helps w/ sticking

Steam for about 5 minutes
steaming gives nice & chewy noodles, but they can stick together quite a bit. You don't HAVE TO use boiling liquid to make the dough for steamed noodles since they are not getting shook-up in water while cooking.

noodles should be eaten warm. when they cool they often become brittle and break up into rice-like bits

COOKED and mashed sweet potato

extruded & dehydrated (eat as is, or partially rehydrate)

mashed staple starch + ripe fruit puree, EXTRUDED & dehydrated to chewy strings

18

RASP cells to a fine paste

(a food processor doesn't work as well to rupture cells.)
(a high powered blender MIGHT work)

the BEST batter for holding BUBBLES!

yam

yep, it is slimy. Don't panic!

cassava

MUSA

sweet potato

Soaked beans, blended into paste

FERMENT batter to get bubbles

the finer you can rasp/grate the batter, the more cohesive the cooked food will be

yam, baked, re-toasted later

FRESHBATTER

If you don't want to go through the trouble of making flour, you can still make great flatbread with grated raw tubers and green bananas.

Loafs can be trickier. They need to be cooked in a container, and the batter should be smooth and thick.

TRY 400°F for 20 min
(cooking times depend on moisture content and how thin you spread the batter.)

BAKE

(likes to stick to pan. Try to get your oil HOT before adding batter, and quickly spread it out.

pan fry

(yam)

TRY 10min cook, flip, cook 5 more min.

pan fry with lid on to steam

(YAM, injera style)

(yam)

(musa)

Try a 10 minute steam for a small muffin. check for doneness.

STEAM

3D breads usually need a container to cook in, and a smooth batter. If batter is too watery it can be difficult to get it to set up. There are way more variables than with using flour, but it can be done. Steaming is easier than baking.
ferment for bubbles.

Sweet potato cooked for a long time into a chewy/crunchy taco shell.

(moist sweet potato freshbatter seems to take the longest time to cook.)

cassava flatbread

CHOP

dehydrate →

MILL
a hand mill with stone grinders is GREAT

but you can also use electric grinders, or even a mortar & pestle

tilt & twirl small blenders while grinding

— fermented cassava

GREEN BANANA
(ever-so-slightly ripe banana makes a sweeter flour, full green is completely starchy.)

YAM

sweet potato

FERMENTED MALANGA

24 hour soaked cowpea flour
I soak → food process into bits → dehydrate. Then grind into flour as needed

LEAF POWDER
(not really a flour, but can be mixed with other flours.)

ARROWROOT STARCH

PRESERVING & MAXIMIZING CALORIES VIA DEHYDRATION/GRINDING
Note: none of these flours is going to perfectly mimic a high gluten wheat flour.*
Also, your flours are going to be highly variable, based on type and grind.
HAVE FUN EXPERIMENTING!

FLOUR

*Hurray! But, if you like wheat, I've found d. alata yam comes closest to mimicking the wheat.

Maranta arundinacea starch extraction

Strain fibers and wash out starch in water

CRUSH RHIZOME

REPEAT

Maranta is the only plant I bother with extracting a pure starch. All other flours are whole.
(except for cassava, yam, and banana peels)

STARCH settles to the bottom, then water is carefully poured off, starch is spread out to fully dry.

STARCH

PRE-GROUND WHOLE RHIZOME
— note excessive fibers

grated WHOLE RHIZOME paste cooked in pan.
WOOL CAKES

THE FINER YOU GRIND THE FLOUR, THE MORE CALORIES CAN BE SQUEEZED OUT AND THE MORE COHESIVE THE COOKED FOOD WILL BE
finely stoneground is topnotch.

bread made with coarsely ground flour.

STORAGE

BEST — Store as WHOLE TUBERS until they break dormancy. Make banana flour once one fruit on bunch turns yellow

OR Store as LARGE DEHYDRATED CHUNKS to reduce surface area exposed to oxygen.

LARGER CHUNKS will have to be broken into smaller bits before grinding

grind into FLOUR as needed

rougher electric grind can be sifted and reground.

BREAD: flour + liquid + gas + heat = DRY FOAM*
(how to make flour edible again)

* a loaf of bread is probably a supernormal tuber

FLOUR + LIQUID + GAS

FLOUR

YAM — finely ground dioscorea alata flour makes a pretty good wheat flour substitute

CASSAVA — I leave the woody core in the flour, making the flour slightly fluffier. Removing the core makes a slightly denser, starchier flour.

BANANA — use mature, but still hard/green fruit for maximum starch. Slightly softer, but still green fruit make a sweeter flour.

SWEET POTATO — this might be the trickiest flour to use for bread & noodles but it is also crazy delicious

LEGUME — an excellent high protein flour, but tends to give everything a kind of BEANY flavor

MARANTA — As a whole flour, this stuff is sawdusty. As a pure starch, it is a bit like glue. You can use it straight but I usually blend it.

MALANGA / TARO — xanthosoma flour has a strong aroma, esp. when fermented. I find it delicious.

CANNA, etc — Please experiment with making flour from other starchy crops!

LIQUID

- water (if you must)
- BROTH / TEA / POTLIKKER / FERMENT BRINE
- aquafaba
- blended mucilaginous leaves
- ripe fruit puree
- fermented ripe fruit puree
- fatty puree / milks (tiger nut, pumpkin seed,) (Avocado gets bitter)
- grated yam

THICK liquid / flour RATIO
1 part flour / 1 part liquid.
✻ These are good starting places. ADJUST as needed depending on what you are making. (see page 22 - CONSISTENCY)

GAS

WILD YEAST / BACTERIA — catch from the air, or edible flowers, fruit, peels

Saved sourdough starter

SAVED YEAST

KEFIR and other edible bacteria / yeast colonies

mechanically whipped foam (carefully fold in flour to maintain bubbles)

fermented "soda" — Sugary juices fermented in a strong container with a pressure release valve make nice bubbly sodas. (I use E-Z CAPS on plastic soda bottles.)

THIN liquid / flour RATIO
1-2 parts flour / 1 part liquid

WATER | AQUAFABA | CASSAVA FLOUR + MALABAR puree + yeast | OPUNTIA puree | RIPE BANANA puree | YAM PUREE

(ALL of these breads taste best warm/hot!)

FLOUR + WATER + YEAST RATIO TESTS. BAKED ON BAKING SHEET WITHOUT CONTAINERS

YAM
- 2f/1w (2/1): Dry, dense, nice crust
- 2f/2w (1/1): nice bread. good crust. moist interior.
- 2f/3w (2/3): great springyness good crust. thick-crust-pizza style
- 2f/1.2w (2/1.2): Pretty much like 2/1. Dry, dense, whole grain wheat flavor.

CASSAVA
- 2f/1.2w (2/1.2): chewy, floury, good interior, floury exterior
- 2f/2w (1/1): a little GUMMY inside, good crust.
- 2f/3w (2/3): nice pizza crust, chewy

400°F for 20 min

BREAD: I generally like a 1/1 flour/water ratio, cooked in a container with walls.

STEAMED cowpea flour
- 5f/2w: too dense, too dry.
- 4f/4w (in a container): SUPER SPONGY moist, quite nice.

GREEN BANANA
- 2f/1w (2/1): like eating a BALL of banana flour. ↑ HOLDS SHAPE, but too dry
- 2f/2w (1/1): MUFFIN-LIKE. ↑ Doesn't hold shape without a container.
- 2f/3w (2/3): Moist interior, dry crust. (maybe a little undercooked) pizza crust.

SEMI-RIPE BANANA
- 2f/1w (2/1): SWEET, cookie-like. sweet plantain flavor.

BREAD
1-2 parts flour + 1 part liquid (cold or pretty hot, but if using yeast don't make it too hot or it will kill your bubblemakers!)

COOKED in a CONTAINER for BEST VOLUME

QUICKBREAD
1 part flour + 1-2 parts liquid. Cooked in a container

BREAD FROM THE FUTURE
4 TBS Flour + 4 TBS liquid + ½ tsp BAKING POWDER* + bit of salt. (mix dry, then liquid) microwave 1 min 30 seconds in a greased ramekin. Eat on your spaceship.

*If you are not growing baking powder, see GAS options on other page.

FLATBREAD
1 part flour + 2 parts liquid* (for batter)
OR
1-2 parts flour + 1 part boiling liquid, dough flattened.

*or even more

NOODLES
1 to 2 parts flour + 1 part liquid. (usually boiling or hot.)
Use a drier mix for dropping into simmering water, or rolling/cutting.
Use a wetter mix for steaming or extruding

SOURDOUGH STARTER

MIX FLOUR + enough water to make a loose batter. (anywhere from 1F/1W to 1F to 2W.) Put somewhere warmish with a cover that keeps out bugs but lets air flow through.

STIR or SHAKE frequently. Wait for **BUBBLES**. Once you get bubbles, you can use it, or if you want a more vigorous starter, feed it 1 TBS FLOUR + 1 TBS water every day until it gets **REALLY BUBBLY**. **REPLACE** what you use with fresh flour/w

JUMPSTART your starter with fruit, peels, dried starter, raw puree of bean/yam/banana/sweet potato, or already fermenting drinks/purees.

DEHYDRATE a **VIGOROUS STARTER** to save yeasts to use later. *at ROOM TEMP, no heat!

CONSISTENCY

ADD FLOUR TO STARTER TO GET THE CONSISTENCY YOU WANT

RUNNY BATTER — use liquidy starter for pancakes / baked flat bread

THICK BATTER — for cooking in a CONTAINER with walls. (or pancakes, flat bread, pizza crust.)

LOOSE STICKY PLAYDOUGH — SHAPED LOAFS (can still benefit from cooking in a container)

PLAYDOUGH — You can shape this anyway you want. Snakes, triangles, flat discs, boxes, etc. BUT it probably won't rise much. Steam it for chewiness, or pan fry in oil for crispy hyperpalatability.

CRUMBLY — make BREAD BITS? or add more liquid and try something else.

⅓ yam ⅓ banana ⅓ cowpea flour (not exactly a fine grind)

1F/1.25W   1F/1W   2F/1.5W

steamed in ramekins for 30 minutes.

nice expansion but not quite fully cooked @ 30 min.

Dense bread

dough too dense to make any air pockets. Bread patty.

MOUTHFEEL

In addition to size & shape & flavor, for maximum hyperpalatability, you will want a wide variety of texture density to entertain the mouth.

CRUNCHY

- dry cooked starch/flour
- FRESH MERISTEM (raw or slightly blanched)
- dry vegetables
- CRUNCHY FRUIT (mostly unripe)
- CRUNCHY TUBERS

SOFT

- WET COOKED VEGETABLES
- COOKED + CRUSHED VEGETABLES
- SOFT RIPE FRUIT
- + liquid or fat

CHEWY

- Steamed/boiled starch/flour
- cooked edible gums/sap
- cooked, then dehydrated sweet potato
- dehydrated sweet fruit

LIQUID

THIN
- BROTH
- JUICE
- BRINE

THICK
- (milks) FAT + WATER
- STARCH + WATER
- PUREE + WATER

SLIMY
- mucilaginous leaf or vegetable puree
- YAM PUREE
- some types of TARO PUREE

GEL

- FRUIT PECTIN
- KEFIR GELS
- LEAF GELS

SUPERNORMAL meat/fruit/tubers. For chewyness I tend to use either starch, sugar, or a combination of the two. Wet cooked starch gets chewy, but loses chewiness when it cools or dries out. Adding some sugar (sweet fruit) helps maintain chewiness. Patties can be made using flour as a binder for leaves/fruit/seeds.
Once I learn my fungi I will add to this category. (mushrooms, tempeh, etc.)

ADD FAT to make CHEWY = MEATY

CHEWY / MEATY / DENSE

Partially dehydrated (sugar)
Ripe fruit, sweet potato, sugar cane juice

STEAMED or boiled flour/starch
Pure starch gets really chewy, but I prefer using it in flour mixes, not on its own.

BOILED/MASHED CASSAVA + mashed ripe banana, dehydrated.

MOCK CHAPATI

1/3 cooked leaves
1/3 boiled yam
1/3 raw ripe banana

BAKED SWEET POTATO dehydrated into chewy jerky

Sweet potato jerky partially rehydrated with a fatty marinade = sweet potato steak

DEHYDRATED into SHEETS, then cooked in oil & spices & a little liquid to rehydrate

Baked pumpkin (including peel) dehydrated + oil + salt = crunchy/chewy hyperpalatable

2 parts cowpea flour + 1 part boiling cactus pad puree + oil, salt, aromatics.

PATTIES
PAN FRIED crispier outside, dense, chewy.
STEAMED like a very dense chewy bread
PAN FRIED WITH LID ON breadly
STEAMED, then PAN FRIED chewy, with excellent browning reaction flavor

FILAMENTS
jackfruit rag
blanched leaves cut into thin strips
1 part flour + 1 part liquid + 1 part filaments
pan fried in oil

SAUCE

A liquid of CONCENTRATED FLAVOR too potent to eat on its own.* Usually very salty, a bit sweet, a bit sour, umami, and very aromatic. Sometimes fatty too, so every note is hit, VERY LOUDLY.

*If your sauce tastes OK to eat on its own, you've probably made a soup. Or you've become normalized to supernormal stimuli. RESET!

aromatic →
- BROTH/TEA infusion
- + FAT infusion
  - COLD OIL soak / massage
  - hot oil toasting in pan
- vinegar infusion
- RAW aromatic

+ FRUIT — Sweet, sour, fermented. Use whatever fruit you have a surplus of.

+ BEANS — Soaked, well cooked, then usually fermented for MAX UMAMI flavor

+ LEAVES — usually combined with oil to make a paste, with salt added to mellow bitterness

+ TUBERS (and starchy fruit) — Cooked & mashed for thick sauce.

+ SEEDS — Soaked, fermented or germinated

+ FLOUR — about 1 TBS flour/cup liquid. Cooked flour thickens sauces. Mixed into cold liquid, then heated to thicken.

+ LACTIC ACID FERMENT OR
- + vinegar
- + acidic fruit or leaf juice

+ SALT — ¼ tsp per cup is a good starting place

BASIC SAUCE
- ¼ cup aromatics paste or 1 TBS powder
- +
- 1 TBS OIL
- +
- ½ tsp salt
- +
- 1 cup SAUCE BASE
- + ½ tsp acidic something if needed.

TEXTURE
- thin broth
- thick soup / cream
- stew
- relish / chutney
- paste, puree
- jam / spread
- jelly
- foam

THINNING
- Strain sauce through various grades of colander, mesh, cloth, etc.
- add more liquid

THICKENING
- cooking down
- mix ½ part flour + ½ cool liquid. Add to sauce and cook until sauce thickens. Don't overcook.

SOUP
All of the above techniques, just a little less concentrated. And larger chunks are more acceptable.

AROMATICS

Plate of aromatics labeled: PERILLA, BASIL, PIPER, SEASONING PEPPERS, BUNCHING ONION, GARLIC CHIVES, PLECTRANTHUS MINT, MARIGOLD, CURRY LEAF, LIPPIA

1/4 cup CHOPPED & BROWNED in 1 TBS oil

1/2 cup fermented ripe banana + 1/2 cup strawberry-guava puree

1 cup

(one example of a) SAUCE

SAUCE BASES such as fruit puree can be dehydrated for storage. Try rehydrating with potlikker!

I like to dehydrate ONE CUP of base per sheet/rollup so I know how much liquid to add to hydrate to original consistency

heated to caramelize some of the sugar + 1/2 tsp salt

BLENDED to a smooth paste (so the fibrous bits of aromatics are not noticeable)

CASSAVA
manihot esculenta

Try and leave roots in the ground until you are ready to process them. (they tend to mold rapidly once dug up.)

PEEL BOTH papery outer & thicker inner peel

Some varieties can be peeled easily, others might need to be cut off with a knife.

for flour and fresh batter, I leave the core in.

WOODY CORE

for boiled or mashed cassava, I remove the core. (it's like toothpicks in your potatoes)

Some roots can become woody all through. I usually compost these, but you might be able to extract starch from them.

I ferment all cassava ★ under water for at least 48 hours, but you can ferment more or less if you like.
The smell gets pretty strong with long ferments, but after dehydrating, the flour smells kind of nice, cheesy.

With unfamiliar varieties, I usually boil a little bit until soft, then do a taste test. If there is any bitterness, I increase the fermentation time for that variety.

★ Low HCN varieties do not need to be fermented, they just need to be fully cooked. I still tend to ferment them anyway.

Baked cassava flour breads can be a bit gummy on the insides sometimes, but with great crusts.

baked, boiled, mashed, fries, chips, flour, fresh batter, bread, flatbread, **NOODLES** bits, balls, crusts, etc. etc.

I prefer STEAMED breads. The crust can be added later via toasting.

YAMS

dioscorea bulbifera — really easy to harvest: just pluck from vine. Good varieties are dense, starchy, delicious. (Now difficult to grow in FL.)

D. alata bulbil (edible, but the main food tuber is underground.)

dioscorea esculenta — delicious, slightly sweet flesh. (But can be bitter close to the peel.)

dioscorea alata — Some varieties are more watery than others. Comes in shades of purple & white. Makes excellent flour.

dioscorea rotundata — Seems like the DENSEST species I've tried. STARCH-PACKED high calorie goodness.

dioscorea pentaphylla — Some varieties produce large bulbils, others concentrate energy on underground storage.

dioscorea polystachya — So far, this species seems to be the least vigorous of the yam species I grow. Tiny bulbils can be cooked like micro potatoes, or the larger underground tuber can be used.

SLIME

Slime is probably the first thing you will notice when you cut into a yam. Some species have more slime than others. Depending on which culture you come from, this might be disconcerting. Don't fret! This slime is actually what gives yams one of their most useful properties: capturing gas in bubbles. This is a great feature when you are trying to make foams like bread. The slime also seems to add an elasticity to doughs and batters that is rather similar to gluten elasticity. The trick to getting a good elastic dough/batter without the end product being slimy is to fully mix the starch cells into the slime. This can be done by making a fine flour, or by rasping the raw yam into a paste with a fine grater. (A blender might work. A food processor doesn't make a smooth mix as well.) The 3rd way to vanish the slime is to cook the yam first, then blend/mash into mashed potato consistency.

OTHER YAMS to try:

dioscorea trifida
dioscorea cayenensis
dioscorea japonica?

Dense fleshed varieties can get pretty dry when baked, but still make great baked french fries. (Use sauce!)

Purple var. of D. alata seems to be ↓ least dense

D. rotundata ← is usually very dense.

Some people are allergic to RAW yam peel, so be careful when peeling not to get the peel on sensitive skin.

DENSITY

Different species/varieties of yam are denser or more watery than others. Denser fleshed types tend to cook dryer, while watery varieties can end up slimy even when fully cooked. If you don't like slime, make mashed yam, fresh batter, or flour.

Some varieties get LARGE

XANTHOSOMA

in some species you can eat the leaves & stems too. COOKED!

main corm

cormels

You can eat the main corm, or leave it in the ground to grow and just harvest the side cormels

Both xanth. & taro plants have tiny needles of calcium oxalate in them that irritate sensitive skin/mouths.

RAPHIDES

FULLY COOKING the corms prevents the raphides from irritating, but apparently the calcium oxalate remains.

To try and reduce the oxalates, I peel, chop up, and ferment before cooking or making flour.

You don't have to, but I like to ferment all xanthosoma under water for 48 to 72 hours. You can also ferment after cooking (like taro cultures making POI) if you are not making flour.

BOIL, STEAM, MASH etc
just make sure you cook completely

BOILED, MASHED, REFRIGERATED to retrograde starch, **CHOPPED** in a food processor into BITS, then dehydrated into **CRUNCHY BITS**

BOILED, MASHED, dehydrated into crispy crackers

BAKED french fries (with oil)
(without oil)

fermented corm → dehydrated → ground into flour → BREAD

*might be tastiest WITHOUT fermentation.

TARO

colocasia esculenta
use pretty much the same way as Xanthosoma. Eat corms, cormels. WATCH OUT FOR RAPHIDES

OVEN BAKED BITS (+oil)
(crunchy outside, soft inside)

COWPEA
VIGNA UNGUICULATA
Please experiment with other edible legumes too!

SOAKING → **24 HOUR SOAK** → **GERMINATED** - possible increase of protein, while reducing carbohydrates. (seems like a waste of calories to me)

BROKEN / FULL SHATTER

BOILED → **BOILED + DEHYDRATED** → **BOILED, partially dried, toasted with oil**

SHATTERED & DEHYDRATED → **FLOUR** → **SOURDOUGH** → **noodles**

FLATBREAD ← **PUREE** → **DEHYDRATED PUREE CRACKER** / **dehydrated noodles**

the liquid left over from boiling beans. **AQUAFABA** Cook down to desired consistency.

FOAM → **RAW PUREE FERMENT** → **steamed IDLI style**

dry cooked in pan + oil DOSA style

MASHED COOKED (with or without fat) (1 to 2 TBS fat/cup beans is really nice)

BOILED BEAN FERMENT with lactic acid bacteria starter.

AQUAFABA + KEFIR soft gel ferment

Leaves

SO MANY EDIBLE SPECIES!

noodle strips (blanched)

WRAPS (raw, blanched, or boiled)

BRINE FERMENTED

* SEE FERMENT PAGE

Crushing & massaging with salt is good for tougher leaves.

Tender leaves work well whole under brine. (1-3 TBS salt/quart.)

Throw in an oak or grape leaf for tannins to keep leaves from getting too mushy.

DEHYDRATED & POWDERED
add to *everything*.

(bread, soup, sauce, drinks, sprinkle like salt on foods.)

(I usually BLANCH first, then spin in a mesh bag, then dehydrate, but this isn't essential unless the species REQUIRES cooking) (I boil chaya 5 min, aroids might need a longer boil to get rid of raphides/oxalates, depending on variety.)

PASTE

typically blended with fat, aromatics, salt.

(a basic pesto is about 1 to 2 TBS oil / packed cup of leaves/aromatics + ¼ tsp salt.)

— DITTO

crispy/crunchy BAKED CHIPS

usually coated in oil

try: DRY leaves + oil Baked @ 300°F about 25 min.

BRINE FERMENTED DEHYDRATED paper chips

Cactus pad puree dehydrated into flakes

OLDER/TOUGHER leaves PRESSURE COOKED

Save cooking water to use for drinks, soups, bread, etc

(IF you know cooking water is SAFE to consume.)

SLIMY LEAF PUREE

(soups, smoothies, bread, dehydrated)

(you might need to add a little liquid to get a smooth blend)

malabar spinach puree dehydrated into wraps

moringa stenopetala

RAW — SUPER-INTENSE. Biting flavor, tough texture.

BLANCHED 30 seconds + rapid cool — Slight crunch, flavorful, delicious.

BOIL 1 min — Still delicious.

BOIL 2 min — Snail parasites killed.

BOIL 3 min — getting tender.

BOIL 5 min — tender, but not yet falling apart. mild flavor.

BOIL 10 min — melt-in-mouth texture. not much flavor.

Pressure Cook 5 min + cooldown — Soft texture, good flavor, good choice for older, tougher leaves.

BROWNED in pan (with oil) — DELICIOUS

CHARRED — CRUNCHY, bitter burned flavor.

BASELLACEAE, MALLOW, CACTUS family, etc.

SLIMY LEAVES
Not being from a culture that appreciates slimy foods, I tend to try and hide the texture in soups, sauces, breads, and dehydrated sheets of leaf puree.

RAW LEAVES
Young & tender leaves of non-poisonous species can be eaten raw, but most improve in flavor with a quick 30 second blanch. (not gynura though)

KATUK shoots might be delicious raw, but I like to at least blanch in boiling water.

BOIL CHAYA SHOOTS at least 5 minutes

Shoots
1.) RAW
2.) 30 second blanch
3.) 5 minute boil

MORINGA STENOPETALA

MORINGA OLEIFERA — good start, horrible aftertaste / SOGGY BUTTER / Fresh crunch, nice!

GYNURA PROCUMBENS — not bad, crunchy. / Still has crunch. not improved / GOOP

COCCINIA GRANDIS — BITTER / CRUNCHY delicious / MUSH

TRICHOSTIGMA OCTANDRUM — medicine flavor / crunchy, intense, good flavor / SOGGY / crunch, slight sweetness, NICE / almost garlic, then horrible

(MORINGA) LEAF CONCENTRATION

ONE PACKED CUP of RAW LEAVES EQUIVALENTS

- 1 packed cup, RAW
- dehydrated (raw)
- 3 TBS RAW POWDER
- BOILED
- dehydrated (boiled)
- 1.5 TBS boiled powder
- BOILED + 2 TBS oil PESTO ½ CUP

※ What about leaf protein concentrate? Why not just rip out the protein instead of eating whole leaves like a gorilla?

Sure. You could do that. But I really like whole foods. You are not just eating for one, you are eating for billions of gut bacteria who really like fiber.

LEAF POWDER
- concentrates protein, minerals, most vitamins. (provided it is dehydrated in the shade at low temperatures. (some loss of vitamin C)

POWDER

whole dried leaves

ONE CUP of Mulberry leaf (morus alba)

※ What about juicing leaves to get all the nutrients without the bulk?
Um. Think of the gut bacteria! Plus, you might not just be concentrating nutrients, You could also be concentrating anti-nutrients. (like the alkaloid papaverine in raw katuk)

PART FOUR
PUTTING IT ALL TOGETHER

1.) Look at your ingredients. Are they nutritionally balanced and diverse? Carry on then.

2.) Design a meal using highly contrasting flavors, textures, and balanced aromatics. Usually this is where the artform of cheffery comes in. But this book is not about that. This book is about brute-force striking of dopamine triggers, giving your primate brain everything it has ever wanted, all at once.* While at the same time sneaking in all its nutritional needs, and avoiding anti-nutrients as much as possible.

*This is what restaurants and junkfood makers do. Of course, you don't really want to become THAT good at making addictive food because it can be hard to not eat excessive amounts. If you do find yourself slipping into crack cocaine meals, RESET TO BASELINE with some plain peasant meals. You'll be fine.

LEAVES

STARCHY TUBER

Sweet & acid fruit

STARCHY FRUIT + fatty seeds

AROMATIC SPICE

AROMATICS

STARCHY FRUIT

SOUR AROMATIC FRUIT

SWEET & starchy fruit

STARCHY SEEDS

CUISINE = NUTRITIONAL BALANCE

ACHIEVE NUTRITIONAL BALANCE THROUGH:

VARIETY: DIVERSITY in a single meal
DIVERSITY between meals
DIVERSITY of kingdoms/species/varieties

So, in a single meal, have some starchy staple, some seeds, some leaves, some fruit, some fat. Probably throw in something fermented and something raw that has vitamin C. (and, you know, something with B12 and iodine would be good too.)

Then, in the next meal, try and eat a different kind of staple, different seeds, leaves, fruit, fermented stuff, and raw vitamin C food (and probably something from the other kingdoms too.) The next meal should be as different as you can make it. There will be seasonal variations, but you can extend your seasons with dehydration and fermentation.

EAT THE MOST DIVERSE DIET YOU CAN GROW WHERE YOU LIVE

Each species and variety is going to provide you with different nutrients. The more diverse you eat, the less likely you will be deficient in any particular nutrient, and the less likely you will be to consume too much of any specific antinutrient. Throw in a bit of animal products to get your B12 and round out your fats, vitamins, minerals and proteins and you should be all right. (and maybe travel to the ocean occasionally to harvest some salt & iodine)

+

HYPERPALATABLE CONTRAST

EVERY FLAVOR EVERY TEXTURE ALL THE TIME

CHEWY, CRUNCHY, STARCHY, FATTY, SWEET, SALTY, SOUR, AROMATIC, PROTEINY, (bitter)
(SPICY HOT, TINGLING, COOL, HOT, EASY TO CHEW AND DIGEST)
in an endless variety of shapes and sizes and layers and packages

THE MORE NOTES YOU HIT, THE MORE DOPAMINE YOU GET
THE MORE DELICIOUS (addictive) THE FOOD IS

The cuisine you make will depend upon what you are growing. I like to dedicate most of my sunlight to growing the staple crops, then the oil crops, then the fruit, and finally the leafy greens, aromatics, and other vegetables. (usually in the dappled shade understory.)

As for individual meals, I tend to go heavy on starches and greens, with some beans, fruit (at least some raw), oil, and seasonal vegetables. If I were growing more oil crops I might go heavier on the fat and greens and lighter on the starches.

I also eat from the animal kingdom, which I have not yet incorporated into the homegarden.

WHATEVER YOU END UP EATING, GO HEAVY ON THE DIVERSITY

Once you get a good balance of nutritional ingredients, you can set about making those ingredients hyperpalatable. So lets say you have some yams, some greens, beans, fruit, oil, and aromatics. There are a gazillion ways you could combine those ingredients into a meal. But if you want a delicious/hyperpalatable meal, try to hit as many of the flavor and mouthfeel notes as you can. You could make the yams soft and salty, the greens crunchy and sour, the beans chewy and spicy, the fruit sweet and sour and silky, and everything fatty. Or you could make the yams crunchy and spicy, the greens soft and fatty, the beans sour, the fruit chewy. You could make a wrap from the yams and fill it with toasted greens, fermented bean paste, a sauce made out of caramelized fruit, oil, and aromatics, with a bit of raw fruit added at the last minute. Or you could make a wrap from the beans and fill it with marinated grilled yam chunks, with a fruit and greens and oil sauce, with a side of raw fruit.

THE POSSIBILITIES ARE PRETTY MUCH ENDLESS.

I usually start designing a meal by figuring out what to do with the staple starch first. (Do I want it to be crunchy? Soft? Chewy? Bread? Bits? All of the above?) Then I figure out how to incorporate as many greens as possible into the meal. (Shall I add greens powder into the flour to make the bread? Or make a fatty greens puree to spread on the bread? Or make a blanched "salad" to go on the side? Or should I use large leaves as a wrap and fill them with fatty mashed tuber?) Then I figure out the legumes. (How about some crunchy roasted beans as a side? Or maybe an oily puree inside the wrap? Or some bean noodles as a filling to a leaf wrap?) Then I figure out the sweet fruit. (Maybe add a little bit to the bread, a little to the greens puree, use some to make a sauce combined with oil and aromatics, and save a little raw to add at the last minute for flavor and vitamin C. Add in whatever other vegetables I can find around the garden, add salt and fat and high temperature browning reactions, a bit of fermented food on the side, and its a meal.

Of course how you go about making your own meals is probably going to be entirely different than the way I go about it.

The food you end up making from your homegarden is going to be unique to you and your homegarden.

With time and experimentation, you will begin to home in on your favorite dishes, and eventually create your own personal HOMEGARDEN CUISINE.

HAPPY FOOD MAKING!

— MARABOU

- loquat/bunching onion/garlic chive/limequat zest salsa
- yam/chaya/katuk/mulberry leaf + cranberry hibiscus powder chips
- cassava "grilled chicken"
- refried yam
- shredded chayote/limequat juice
- banana/cassava tortilla

D'ALATA YAM CRUST

PAPAYA JUNEPLUM LIMEQUAT GARLIC CHIVE SAUCE

SEASONING PEPPER & Betel leaf topping

The George Washington Carver
- sweet potato flour bun
- sweet potato leaf
- sweet potato patty

- dioscorea esculenta
- fermented seasoning peppers
- fermented tindora
- malabar spinach wrap (dehydrated purée)

Made in the USA
Columbia, SC
11 November 2017